NUMBERS

by Philip Carona

pictures by Mary Gehr

CHILDRENS PRESS • CHICAGO

Childrens Press is grateful to Margaret Matchett,
Mathematics Consultant, Laboratory School, Univer-
sity of Chicago, for her gracious criticism and advice.

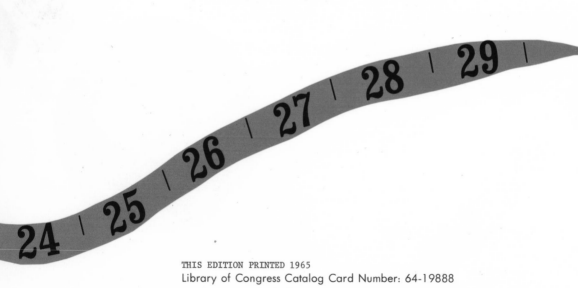

THIS EDITION PRINTED 1965
Library of Congress Catalog Card Number: 64-19888

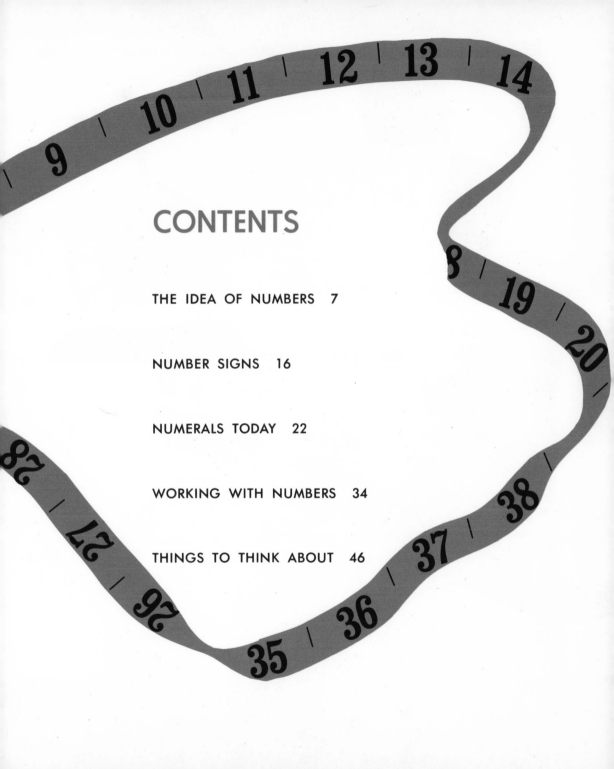

CONTENTS

THE IDEA OF NUMBERS

We use numbers every day.
Try to count the ways we
use numbers and number signs.

may

s	m	t	w	t	f	s
			1	2	3	4
5	6	7	8	9	10	11

People have not always
used numbers as we do.

The town of Elko, Nevada,
may have gotten its name from
an Indian number word.

"Elko" meant "one woman."

The Indians saw many white
men coming. They had just a
few women with them.

"Elko," said the Indians.

This was the Indian way
of saying that there were
few women.

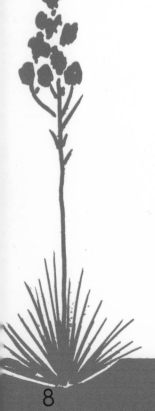

An Indian hunter who saw
a hundred buffaloes might say,
"Buffalo spring up like grass
in the prairie." This was his
way of saying there were many
buffaloes for the hunters.

Long, long ago a cave man
may have had two spears.

Perhaps he saw two
elephants.

He could see that two
spears and two elephants
were different. Yet he
may have seen that they
were alike in one way.

Perhaps he was beginning
to get the idea of TWO.

13

One day he might see
one group of animals on
a hill. There might be
another group of animals
by the river. TWO groups.

The cave man did not have
a word or a number sign for
the idea of two.

If he killed two elephants,
he might paint two elephants
on the cave wall. This was
the way he told how many he
had killed.

NUMBER SIGNS

People who began to understand the idea of numbers used number signs.

Many different number signs have been used.

Here are some of the number signs that were used in Egypt.

ONE

TEN

ONE HUNDRED

ONE THOUSAND

TEN THOUSAND

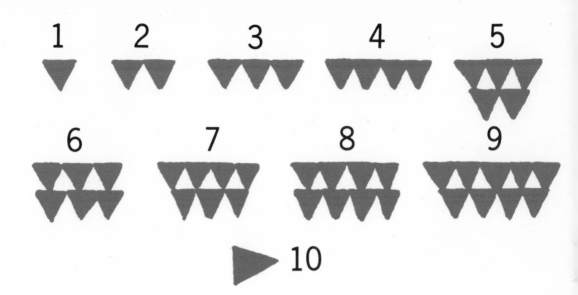

1 2 3 4 5
6 7 8 9
10

The people of Mesopotamia
made number signs in soft clay
with a pointed stick.

一 1
二 2
三 3
四 4
五 5

十 10

The Chinese painted number
signs with a brush.

The Romans made number signs, numerals, that are still used sometimes today.

The numerals for one, two and three were just lines.

I   II   III

For five they used V.

For ten they used X.

For fifty they used L.

Four is one less than five.

Eleven is one more than ten.

V
X
L
IV
XI

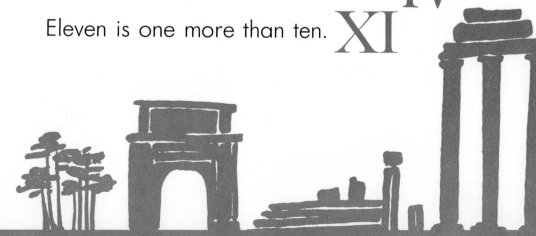

For larger numbers, the Romans used the first letter of Latin words. The Romans spoke Latin.

The Latin word for hundred is Centum. The letter used for hundred was C

The Latin word for thousand is Mille. So the letter used for thousand was M

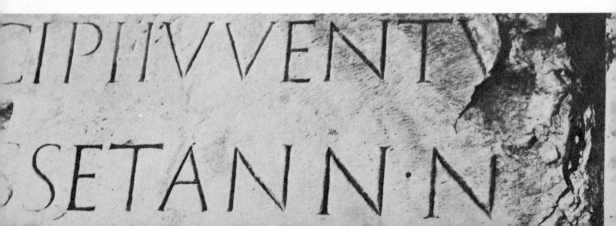

Here are some Roman numerals.

I II III IV V VI VII

VIII IX X XI XX

XXX   CCC

M   one thousand

CM   nine hundred

LX   sixty (fifty and ten)

IV   four (one less than five)

MXL   one thousand forty

It is not hard to read Roman
numerals, but they are clumsy
to use.

MCMXIV • 1914

NUMERALS TODAY

Numerals we use look like this:

1 2 3 4 5 6 7 8 9 0

Where did they come from?

Long before the Romans were
using letters to express number
ideas, people in India were
writing numerals. They looked
like this:

1 2 3 4 5 6 7 8 9

The people were called Hindus,
and they had nine number signs.

With nine number signs the
Hindus could write any numeral.
   These numerals were not clumsy.
   They were easy to read.
   They were easy to work with.
   If a man wanted to buy three
sheep he wrote it this way:

$$3$$ (3 ones)

   If he wanted to buy thirty-three
sheep he wrote it this way.

$$3\ 3$$

(3 tens and 3 ones)

   Each three had a "place value."

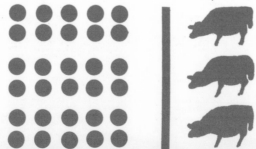

If he wanted to buy three hundred and thirty three sheep, he wrote it this way:

333

(3 hundreds   3 tens   3 ones)

If he wanted a 3 to mean 3 tens instead of 3 ones, he moved it one space to the left.

When he moved his 3 another space to the left, it meant 3 hundreds.

He had a number pattern.

It was based on ten.

25

How could he write three
hundred and three?

There were no tens.

He left a space and wrote
it this way:

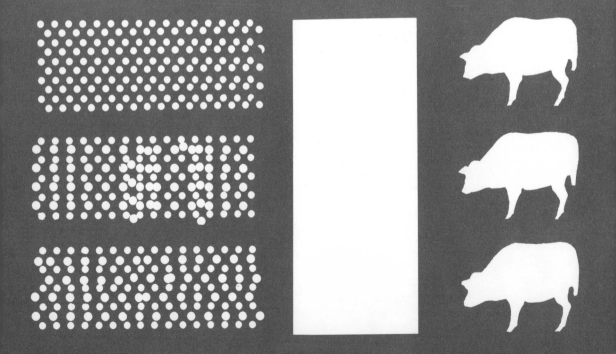

This sometimes led to
trouble. If a man wanted
three hundred and three sheep
and wrote a 3 3, he might get
only thirty three because his
numeral was hard to read.

As time went on, the Hindus began using a dot where there were no elements — nothing — in a column. They wrote 3 • 3 and this was better.

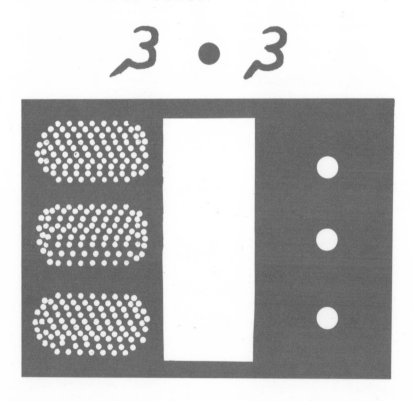

Later this small dot became
a circle. The circle is now
called ZERO.

The numeral zero was one of the
world's great inventions.

Zero is the number sign which
means no objects, no quantity.

1•

:4:

:2

3:•

The Hindus were traders.
When they traveled they took
both goods and ideas with them.
They shared their number ideas
with the Arabs.

The Arabs carried the ideas farther west. Spain began to use the ten number signs and place value. The numerals were called Arabic numerals. Soon they were used all over Europe.

The shape of the numerals changed many times.

Then, about six hundred years ago, printing was invented.

The shape that numerals took at that time was kept.

These are the numerals that we use today.

We call them Arabic numerals.

1234567890

WORKING WITH NUMBERS

Wise men of long ago found a way to work with numbers without using any numerals, or number signs.

They worked with an abacus. The word abacus comes from the Latin word abax which means tablet.

The early abacus was made by drawing three lines in the sand. Pebbles were placed in the lines.

The pebbles can show
six hundred and thirty seven
when placed this way.

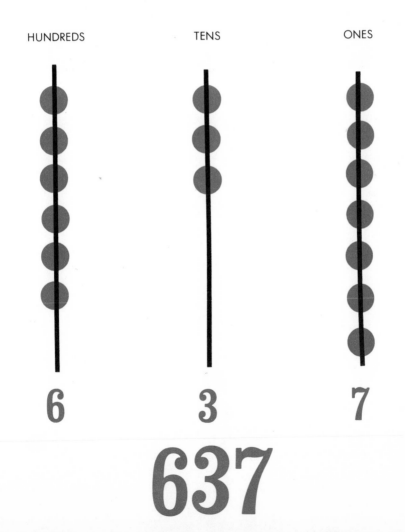

HUNDREDS TENS ONES

6 3 7

637

Suppose a man had 231 camels and he wanted to buy 125 more. How many camels would he have? He set his pebbles so they showed 231.

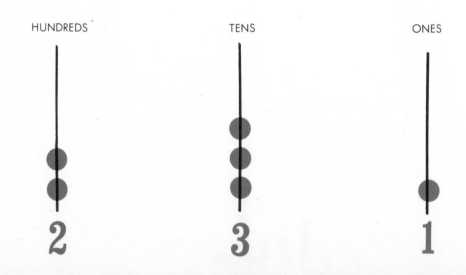

HUNDREDS	TENS	ONES
2	3	1

Then he put five pebbles on the line for ones. He put two pebbles on the line for tens. He put one pebble on the line for hundreds.

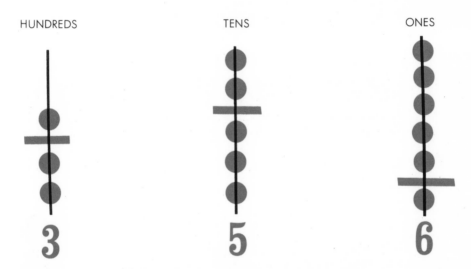

HUNDREDS TENS ONES

3 5 6

Then he could see that he would have 356 camels.

He had three hundred and
fifty six camels.

Now he had more camels than
he could use. He sold forty-five
of them. How many did he have left?

When he sold 45 of them, he took
five pebbles from the line for ones.
He took four pebbles from the line
for tens. He could see that he had
311 camels left.

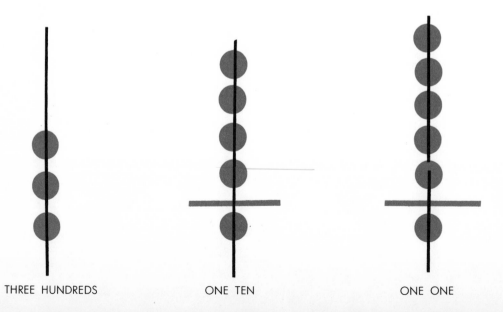

THREE HUNDREDS   ONE TEN   ONE ONE

The Chinese use an abacus
that has colored beads. The
beads can be moved back and forth
on rods.

Even today, some Chinese
use an abacus when they are
working with numbers.

A boy has three rabbit cages.

There are four rabbits in
one cage.

There are three rabbits in
one cage.

There are no rabbits in one
cage.

How does he find out how many
rabbits he has?

He can put them all together
and count the rabbits.

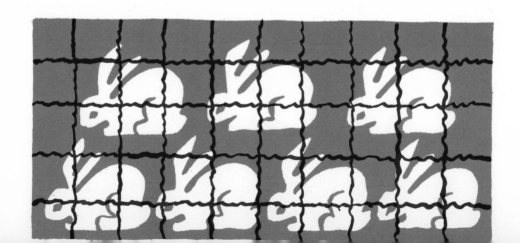

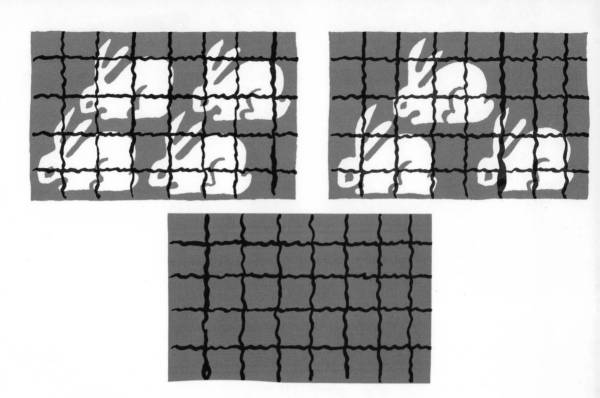

Or he can work with numbers.

He can say 3 and 4 are 7.

He can say 4 and 3 are 7.

He can say 3 and 4 and 0 are 7.

He can say 0 and 4 and 3 are 7.

Zero is a wonderful numeral.

It means there are no objects

in a group.

We use numbers every day.
They tell us how far, how fast,
how much, how many, how tall.

We work with numbers every day

. . . if we bake a cake . . .

play a game . . . keep a score.

43

Men work with numbers when
they build a bridge . . .
or design a jet . . .